WHILE

CAMPING

CAMPING JOURNAL FOR KIDS

This
CAMPING JOURNAL
belongs to

Camp Trip Dates

Month..................

SUN	MON	TUE	WED	THU	FRI	SAT

Notes

....

....

....

Schedule

Day 1

Day 2

Day 3

Day 4

Days Until We Go

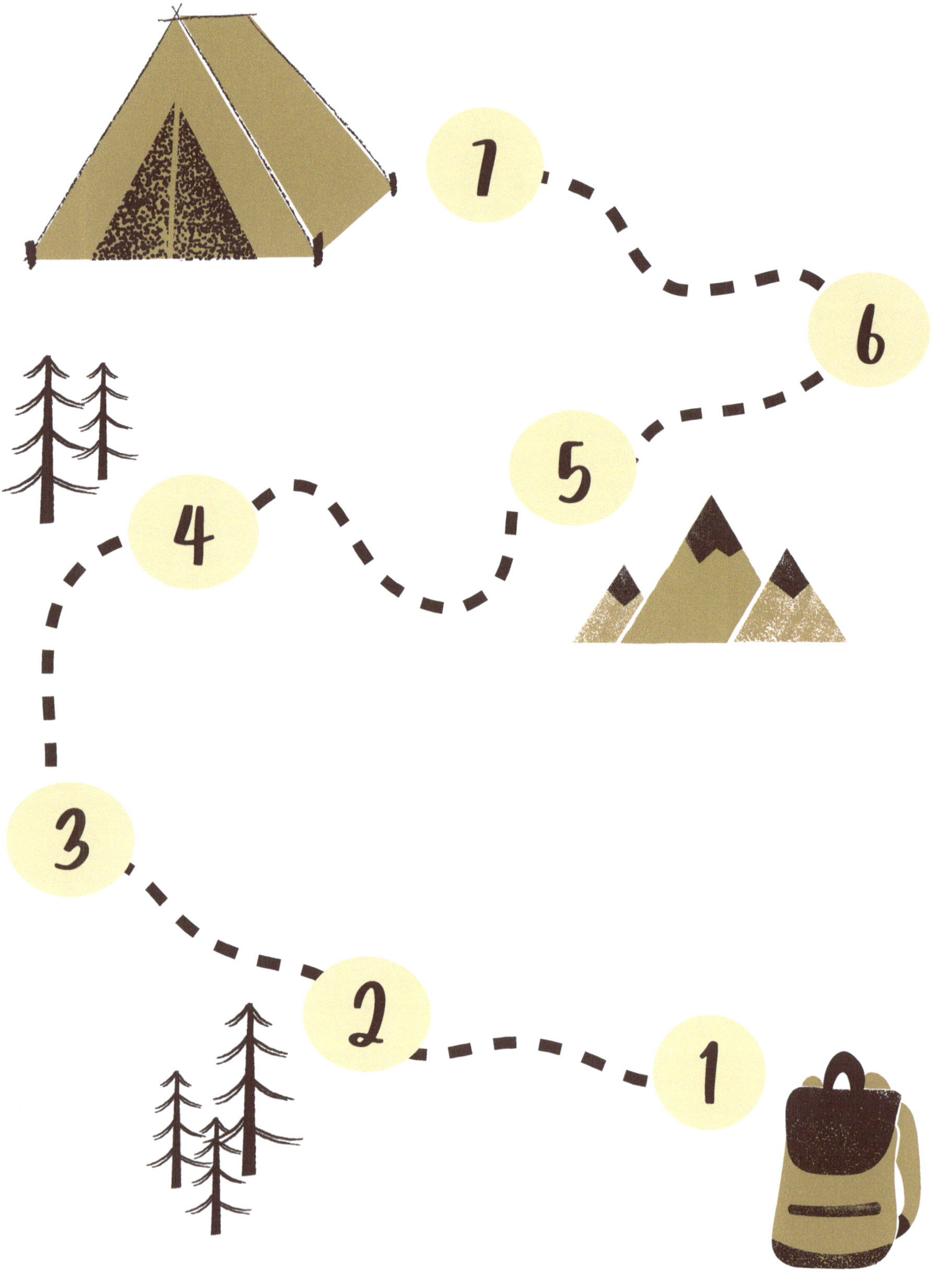

7
6
5
4
3
2
1

Bucket List

things I want to SEE, DO, & LEARN

Camp Rules

- ✓ No eating in the tent
- ✓ Respect the fire
- ✓ Always wear your whistle
- ✓ Never go barefoot
- ✓ Keep horseplay to a minimum
- ✓ Always stick with a buddy
- ✓ No snacking on mushrooms and berries
- ✓ No petting the wildlife
- ✓ Be on time for all scheduled activities
- ✓ Respect the personal property of others
- ✓ Respect your neighbors

Map

DRAW YOUR CAMPSITE

Activity #1

ABC'S SCAVENGER HUNT

- [ ] A - Ant
- [ ] B - Bark
- [ ] C - Creek
- [ ] D - Dew
- [ ] E - Evergreen tree
- [ ] F - Flower
- [ ] G - Green leaf
- [ ] H - Hat
- [ ] I - Insect in a web
- [ ] J - Jug of water
- [ ] K - Kindling
- [ ] L - Lady bug
- [ ] M - Map
- [ ] N - Nest
- [ ] O - Orange leaf
- [ ] P - Pinecone
- [ ] Q - Quick animal
- [ ] R - Rock
- [ ] S - Sunglasses
- [ ] T - Tree Stump
- [ ] U - Unique Rock
- [ ] V - "V" shape in tree
- [ ] W - Walking stick
- [ ] X - "X" on the map
- [ ] Y - "Y" shaped stick
- [ ] Z - Zipper

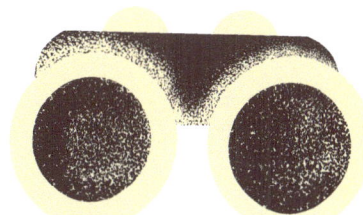

Activity 2

B I N G O

Built a tent	Find a colorful bird	Pack for camp	Have a picnic	Relax outside
Help make a dinner	Scavenger hunt	Stargazing	Roast a marshmallow	Go on a hike
Collect different types of leaves	Camp fire	FREE	Play I-Spy	Make s'mores
look for wildlife	tell stories in the dark	Find animal tracks	Find water	Learn something about nature
Sing a camp song	Read a book in the shade	Read the map	Look for bugs	Play a sport

Activity #3

SUMMER CAMP WORD SEARCH

p	k	v	v	s	u	n	s	c	r	e	e	n	t	x
y	p	k	c	b	k	i	p	g	y	j	z	t	n	b
r	k	a	s	e	s	s	a	l	g	n	u	s	e	i
s	m	o	v	v	s	p	u	z	o	k	j	d	t	s
t	e	h	s	m	i	e	o	y	w	v	i	v	b	f
w	h	r	m	m	y	g	m	v	x	t	b	g	d	w
x	g	c	i	t	o	g	t	o	c	r	l	t	i	q
a	l	j	a	f	s	r	w	l	l	a	q	e	m	s
l	e	m	x	e	p	d	e	e	p	v	v	u	k	r
e	u	q	s	t	b	m	k	s	n	e	q	j	h	h
r	f	l	a	y	w	i	a	u	x	l	a	v	p	y
r	f	j	i	d	h	i	s	c	i	e	l	m	m	q
m	n	g	n	q	o	f	r	j	p	s	w	f	a	n
s	w	i	m	w	e	a	r	z	s	d	q	g	c	d
o	i	e	q	x	d	t	x	n	t	n	i	w	a	c

beach   travel   sunscreen   swimwear

tent   camp   campfire   hike

sunglasses   s'mores   sun   relax

Activity #4

TIC TAC TOE

Activity #4

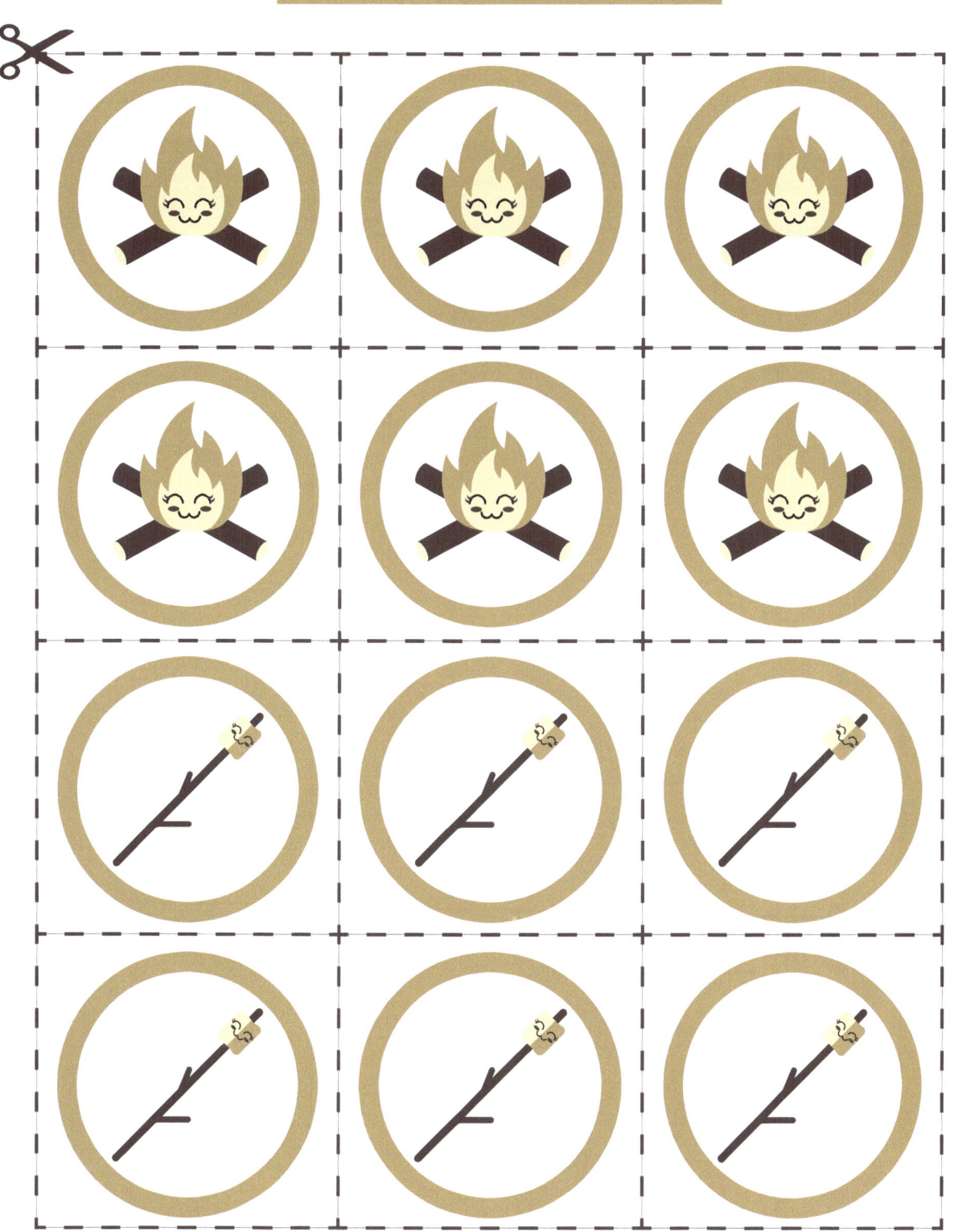

Activity #5

CAMP CHARADES

Chopping firewood	Making a campfire	Act like a fish
Blowing out a S'mores fire	Pounding a tent stake in	Having a hard time setting up the tent
Blowing bubbles	Putting on bug spray	Ah! Bug spray in my eyes!
Skipping stones	Reeling in a big fish	Seeing a big bear walk in front of you
Act like a bear	Act like a moose	Act like a chipmunk
Hiking up a steep mountain	Swimming in a lake	Going to sleep in your sleeping bag

Day #_____

weather

Date ....

Mon tue Wed thu Fri Sat Sun

things I learned today

....
....
....
....
....

today I ate

....
....

Day # _____

weather | **Date** ....
 | Mon tue Wed thu Fri Sat Sun

things I learned today

....
....
....
....
....

today I ate

....
....

Day #_____

weather

Date ....

Mon tue Wed thu Fri Sat Sun

things I learned today

....
....
....
....
....

today I ate

....

....

Day #_____

weather

Date ....
Mon tue Wed thu Fri Sat Sun

things I learned today

....
....
....
....
....

today I ate

....

....

Day #_____

weather	Date ....
☀ ⛅ 🌬 🌧 ⛈	Mon tue Wed thu Fri Sat Sun

things I learned today

....

....

....

....

....

today I ate

....

....

Best Camp Food

Memories

Location : .... Date : ....

[ATTACH PHOTO HERE]

About this photo ....
....
....
....
....

that's A Wrap

Would you go back? ☐ Yes ☐ No

the best part was

....
....
....
....
....

What would you want to visit next?

....
....
....
....
....

New Friends

Name:
Phone:
Address:
Email:
Birthday:
Notes:

Name:
Phone:
Address:
Email:
Birthday:
Notes:

Name:
Phone:
Address:
Email:
Birthday:
Notes:

Notes

Copyright© 2022 by Bookfly Publishing

No part of this publication may be reproduced, stored in a retrieval system, or transmitted in any form or by any means, electronic, mechanical, photocopying, recording, or otherwise, without the written permission of the publisher. Limited Liability/Disclaimer of Warranty. The publisher and the author make no representation or warranties with the respect to the accuracy or completeness of the contents of this work and specifically disclaim all warranties including without limitation warranties for a particular purpose. No warranty may be created or extended by sales or promotional materials. The advice or strategies contained herein may not be suitable for every situation. This work is sold with the understanding that the publisher is not engaged in rendering medical, legal, or other professional advice or services. Neither the publisher nor the author or creator shall be liable for damages arising.

For general information on our other products and services please visit www.bookflypublishing.com or contact our Customer Care Department at info@bookflypublishing.com.
Bookfly Publishing publishes its books and materials in a variety of electronic and print formats. Some content that appears in print may not be available in electronic books and vice versa.

Cover: Uliana Barabesh
ISBN 978-1-7369393-4-5
All rights reserved. Published by Bookfly Publishing
Harvey, Louisiana
www.bookflypublishing.com

Printed in the USA

www.ingramcontent.com/pod-product-compliance
Lightning Source LLC
Chambersburg PA
CBHW050747110526
44590CB00003B/103